CONTINENTS OF THE WORLD

DISCOVERING
SOUTH
AMERICA'S
LAND, PEOPLE, AND WILDLIFE

A MyReportLinks.com Book

David Schaffer

 MyReportLinks.com Books

an imprint of

Enslow Publishers, Inc.

Box 398, 40 Industrial Road
Berkeley Heights, NJ 07922
USA

To Helena and Lily Jane—
may what I do help you to learn well.

MyReportLinks.com Books, an imprint of Enslow Publishers, Inc. MyReportLinks®
is a registered trademark of Enslow Publishers, Inc.

Library of Congress Cataloging-in-Publication Data

Schaffer, David.
  Discovering South America's land, people, and wildlife / David Schaffer.
    p. cm. — (Continents of the world)
  Includes bibliographical references and index.
  ISBN 0-7660-5208-7
  1. South America—Juvenile literature. [1. South America.] I. Title. II. Series.
  F2208.5.S44 2004
  980—dc22

                        2003026716

Printed in the United States of America

10 9 8 7 6 5 4 3 2 1

To Our Readers:
Through the purchase of this book, you and your library gain access to the Report Links that specifically back
up this book.
The Publisher will provide access to the Report Links that back up this book and will keep these Report Links
up to date on **www.myreportlinks.com** for three years from the book's first publication date.
We have done our best to make sure all Internet addresses in this book were active and appropriate when we
went to press. However, the author and the Publisher have no control over, and assume no liability for, the
material available on those Internet sites or on other Web sites they may link to.
The usage of the MyReportLinks.com Books Web site is subject to the terms and conditions stated on the
Usage Policy Statement on **www.myreportlinks.com**.
A password may be required to access the Report Links that back up this book. The password is found on the
bottom of page 4 of this book.
Any comments or suggestions can be sent by e-mail to comments@myreportlinks.com or to the address on
the back cover.

Photo Credits: AP/Wide World Photos, p. 40; Artville (map); © 1995–2004 Public Broadcasting
Service (PBS), pp. 13, 36; © 2000–04 The Metropolitan Museum of Art, pp. 27, 33, 35; © Corel
Corporation, pp. 3, 9, 16, 18, 20, 23, 24, 28, 30, 31, 43, 45; © The Rector and Visitors of the
University of Virginia, p. 14; GeoAtlas, p. 11; MyReportLinks.com Books, p. 4; The World of Tribal
Arts, p. 38.

Cover Photos: Artville (map); Clipart.com; Photos.com.

Contents

MyReportLinks.com Books
Great Books, Great Links, Great for Research!

The Report Links listed on the following four pages can save you hours of research time by **instantly** bringing you to the best Web sites relating to your report topic.

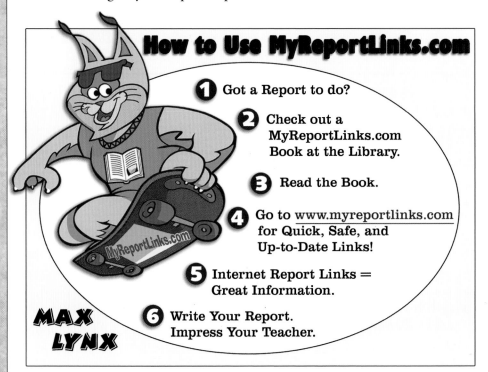

How to Use MyReportLinks.com

1 Got a Report to do?

2 Check out a MyReportLinks.com Book at the Library.

3 Read the Book.

4 Go to www.myreportlinks.com for Quick, Safe, and Up-to-Date Links!

5 Internet Report Links = Great Information.

6 Write Your Report. Impress Your Teacher.

MAX LYNX

The pre-evaluated Web sites are your links to source documents, photographs, illustrations, and maps. They also provide links to dozens—even hundreds—of Web sites about your report subject.

MyReportLinks.com Books and the MyReportLinks.com Web site save you time and make report writing easier than ever!

Please see "To Our Readers" on the copyright page for important information about this book, the MyReportLinks.com Web site, and the Report Links that back up this book. Please enter **CSA6406** if asked for a password.

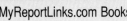

Report Links

The Internet sites described below can be accessed at http://www.myreportlinks.com

*EDITOR'S CHOICE

▶**Country Information**
This Web site from the Bureau of Western Hemisphere Affairs contains information on the countries located in this region of the world, including those in South America.

*EDITOR'S CHOICE

▶*Journey into Amazonia*
Journey into Amazonia, a PBS series, explores the Amazon's sacred ground, plants, animals, and more.

*EDITOR'S CHOICE

▶*The Encyclopedia of World History:* **South America**
At the Bartleby Web site you will find a time line of South America's history.

*EDITOR'S CHOICE

▶**Perry-Castañeda Library Map Collection: Maps of the Americas**
The Perry-Castañeda Library holds a collection of maps of South America.

*EDITOR'S CHOICE

▶**Andes Mountains**
Learn about the animals, plants, and climate of the Andes Mountains.

*EDITOR'S CHOICE

▶**South America**
Explore South America at this Web site. By clicking on a country you will find a detailed description of that country and a picture of its flag.

Report Links

The Internet sites described below can be accessed at
http://www.myreportlinks.com

▶**Adventures in South America**

At the Adventures in South America Web site there is information about Cuzco, the Inca Trail, Machu Picchu, and much more.

▶**Biography**

The official Evita Perón Web site contains biographical information and photos of the former first lady of Argentina.

▶**Civilizations in America**

The Civilizations in America Web site provides information about many different cultures, including the Inca and the Chavin.

▶*Conquistadors*

Conquistadors, a PBS Web site, explores the lives of Hernán Cortés, Francisco Pizarro, Francisco de Orellana, and Alvar Núñez Cabeza de Vaca.

▶**Country at a Glance**

Country at a Glance, a United Nations Cyberschoolbus Web site, provides descriptions of countries in South America.

▶**Country Studies**

The Library of Congress Web site provides a detailed history of countries in South America, including Brazil, Peru, Argentina, Colombia, and Ecuador.

▶**El Libertador**

This site houses a biography of Simón Bolívar. He helped lead the South American fight for independence from colonial rulers.

▶**Fact Monster: Tropic of Capricorn**

At the Fact Monster Web site you will find a brief description of the Tropic of Capricorn. This imaginary line is found on maps and globes at about 23.5 degrees latitude south of the equator.

Report Links

The Internet sites described below can be accessed at http://www.myreportlinks.com

▶ **Galápagos**

This Web site lets readers explore the Galápagos Islands. They can learn about the history of the islands and view a slide show.

▶ **Heroes & Icons: Pelé**

This *Time* magazine article is about soccer legend Pelé. Read about his life and career, as well as his impact on the game of soccer.

▶ **Ice Treasures of the Inca**

Ice Treasures of the Inca, a *National Geographic* Web site, takes readers on an adventure leading to the discovery of a mummified Inca girl.

▶ **Incas & Conquistadors**

This Web site provides information about the Spanish conquest of the Inca. You will also learn about the Inca Empire, the Spanish conquistadors, and Inca ruins.

▶ **The Jorge Luis Borges Collection**

Learn about Jorge Luis Borges, a well-known author from Argentina. Information about his life and works is included.

▶ **The Kota Mama Expedition**

The Kota Mama Expedition Web site tells the story of those who set out on an expedition to prove that ancient people used traditional boats to navigate South American waterways.

▶ **Lonely Planet: Destinations**

The Lonely Planet Web site contains general information about countries in South America.

▶ **Nationalgeographic.com: Map Machine**

Find profiles of many countries in South America at the nationalgeographic.com: Map Machine Web site. There are printable maps as well.

Report Links

The Internet sites described below can be accessed at http://www.myreportlinks.com

▶*Nova: Ice Mummies*

Nova: Ice Mummies follows a 1996 Peruvian expedition to Mount Sara Sara. Read about the archaeologists' exciting findings.

▶Rain of the Moon: Silver in Ancient Peru

At the Metropolitan Museum of Art Web site users can explore ancient Peruvian art and artifacts.

▶Secrets of Easter Island

The Secrets of Easter Island, a PBS Web site, explores Easter Island, its first inhabitants, and megaliths.

▶The Spirit of Ancient Peru

There is an abundance of tribal art at the Spirit of Ancient Peru Web site. View images of the various collections, and learn about their cultural significance.

▶South American Civilizations: The Moche and Inca

Explore early civilizations of South America, including the Inca and the Moche. Learn which places are important to the history of each group of people.

▶South American Sites and Culture

At the South American Sites and Culture Web site you will learn about the Inca, Chimu, Nazca, and other cultures.

▶Unknown Amazon

The British Museum allows people to view artifacts from the Amazonian region of South America.

▶*The World Factbook*

At the CIA's *The World Factbook* Web site you can explore countries in South America by choosing a country from the drop-down menu.

South America Facts

Area

6,898,579 square miles
   (17,867,320 square meters)

Population*

355,068,000

Five Most
Populous Cities*

São Paulo, Brazil
   (17,962,000)
Buenos Aires, Argentina
   (12,106,000)
Rio de Janeiro, Brazil
   (10,652,000)
Lima, Peru (7,594,000)
Bogotá, Colombia
   (6,957,000)

Highest Point
of Elevation

Mount Aconcagua
   (in Argentina)
   22,834 feet
   (6,960 meters)

Lowest Point
of Elevation

Peninsula Valdés, Argentina
   131 feet below sea level
   (−40 meters)

Major Mountain
Ranges

Andes, Canastra, Cordoba,
Espinhaco, Guiana
Highlands

Major Lakes

Poopó, Mar Chiquita,
Maracaibo, Mirim, Titicaca

Major Rivers

Amazon, Araguaia, Japurá,
Madeira, Magdelena,
Negro, Orinoco, Paraguay,
Paraná, Pilcomayo, Purus,
Putomayo, Río de la Plata,
São Francisco, Tocantins,
Uruguay, Xingu

Countries

Argentina, Bolivia, Brazil,
Chile, Colombia, Ecuador,
Guyana, Paraguay, Peru,
Suriname, Uruguay,
Venezuela

Rio de Janeiro ▶

*Population estimates from 2002 as recorded in
The World Almanac and Book of Facts 2003.

9

A Colorful Place

South America is a peninsula located mostly in the Southern Hemisphere, between the Atlantic and Pacific Oceans. It covers almost 7 million square miles (18 million square kilometers) and is the fourth largest continent. South America extends farther south than any other continent except Antarctica. Twelve nations and two colonies, one French and one British, make up South America.

The earliest South Americans were American Indians. The Inca, a highly advanced early civilization, were located in South America. They controlled an empire of between 9 million and 16 million people, but they were conquered by Spanish soldiers known as *conquistadors* in the early sixteenth century.[1] Spain has had enormous influence on South America. Spanish is the official language in all but three South American countries. Yet in the largest nation in South America, Brazil, the official language is Portuguese.

▶ Distinguishing Characteristics

South America is known worldwide for its people's colorful dress, festive decorations and holiday celebrations, and spicy, zesty food. Fine quality sculpture, architecture, and handcrafts have been produced in South America. Mosaics, art made from small pieces of stone or other material, are especially common there. Many buildings have mosaics built into their walls.

CARIBBEAN SEA

Caracas

Orinoco River

VENEZUELA   Georgetown
                GUYANA   Paramaribo
Bogotá   Cayenne
                    SURINAME FRENCH
COLOMBIA   GUIANA

ECUADOR
        Quito
Galápagos   Amazon River
Islands
                Amazon River

Lima
                            BRAZIL
PERU   **BOLIVIA**
                            Brasília
Lake Titicaca
PACIFIC   La Paz
OCEAN   Lake Poopó

                PARAGUAY

CHILE   São Paulo   Rio de Janeiro
                Asunción
        Andes Mountains

                Mt.Aconcagua   **ATLANTIC**
                22,834 feet   **OCEAN**
                (6,960 meters)   Porto Alegre
Santiago   **URUGUAY** Rio Grande
            Buenos
            Aires   Montevideo

        ARGENTINA

                Falkland Islands

        Tierra del Fuego

            Cape Horn

▲ *A world map of South America.*

South American music is also popular worldwide. Music and dance styles such as the tango, samba, and bossa nova all originated in South America. Samba music is the featured entertainment at Brazil's most festive holiday celebration, Carnival. Carnival marks the beginning of the Christian religious period known as Lent. Brazilian Carnival celebrations are famous for their color and flair.

With a mostly tropical or subtropical climate, South America is also well known for growing fruits, including bananas, mangoes, and coconuts. Many tree nuts such as pistachios are produced in South America and shipped worldwide. Coffee, grain, wine, sheep, and cattle are also major South American agricultural products.

Mineral mining has been a big industry since the first Spanish settlers came. Gold and diamonds have been mined heavily in the mountains of South America. Copper, iron ore, and steel are also major parts of the South American mining industry.

▶ The World's Largest Rain Forest

An especially unique and important region in South America is the Amazon River basin and rain forest. This is the world's largest tropical rain forest. Plants and trees from the rain forest produce gases needed by the earth's atmosphere. Rain forest plants also provide important ingredients for many medicines. Recently, the rain forest has been reduced and threatened by the cutting of trees, oil production, mining, road construction, and the spread of farmlands. The whole world has taken notice of these problems, but a solution has yet to be found. History professor John Charles Chasteen claims, "Latin America's best known, largest-scale environmental issues concern the Amazon rain forest."[2]

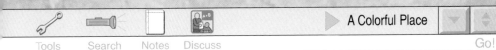
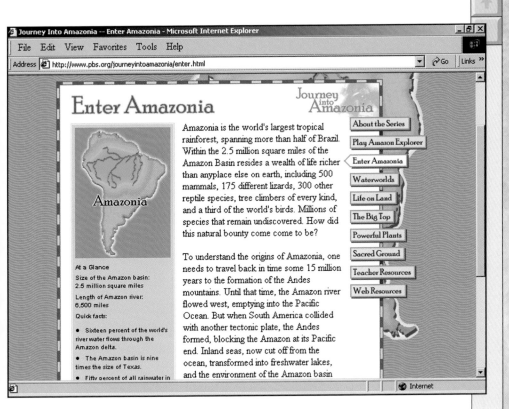

Journey Into Amazonia -- Enter Amazonia - Microsoft Internet Explorer

File Edit View Favorites Tools Help

Address http://www.pbs.org/journeyintoamazonia/enter.html

Enter Amazonia

Journey into Amazonia

Amazonia is the world's largest tropical rainforest, spanning more than half of Brazil. Within the 2.5 million square miles of the Amazon Basin resides a wealth of life richer than anyplace else on earth, including 500 mammals, 175 different lizards, 300 other reptile species, tree climbers of every kind, and a third of the world's birds. Millions of species that remain undiscovered. How did this natural bounty come come to be?

To understand the origins of Amazonia, one needs to travel back in time some 15 million years to the formation of the Andes mountains. Until that time, the Amazon river flowed west, emptying into the Pacific Ocean. But when South America collided with another tectonic plate, the Andes formed, blocking the Amazon at its Pacific end. Inland seas, now cut off from the ocean, transformed into freshwater lakes, and the environment of the Amazon basin

Amazonia

At a Glance
Size of the Amazon basin:
2.5 million square miles

Length of Amazon river:
6,500 miles

Quick facts:

- Sixteen percent of the world's river water flows through the Amazon delta.

- The Amazon basin is nine times the size of Texas.

- Fifty percent of all rainwater in

About the Series
Play Amazon Explorer
Enter Amazonia
Waterworlds
Life on Land
The Big Top
Powerful Plants
Sacred Ground
Teacher Resources
Web Resources

Internet

At 2.5 million square miles, the Amazon River basin is nine times larger than the state of Texas.

People and Events of South American History

Many government and military leaders have been important to the history of South America. The Inca ruler Topa Inca Yupanqui led the Inca Empire to the height of its power. The Spanish conqueror Francisco Pizarro led the fabled conquistadors who defeated the Inca and won control of much of South America for Spain. Simón Bolívar became a hero by leading the war against Spain for South American independence in the early nineteenth century.

More recently, government leaders in some major South American countries have been famous, or infamous,

for their actions and policies. Argentine President Juan Perón and his wife, Evita, led their nation in the 1940s and 1950s. They sought to improve economic conditions for Argentina's poor and working classes. Evita Perón had once been poor herself. She was so loved by working-class Argentineans and fascinating to others that a Broadway play and Hollywood movie were made about her life. In the 1970s and 1980s, Chile was ruled by General Augusto Pinochet Ugarte. Pinochet's government became known for its harsh rule and oppression of opponents. Conflicts between rich and poor classes have also played a large role in South American history.

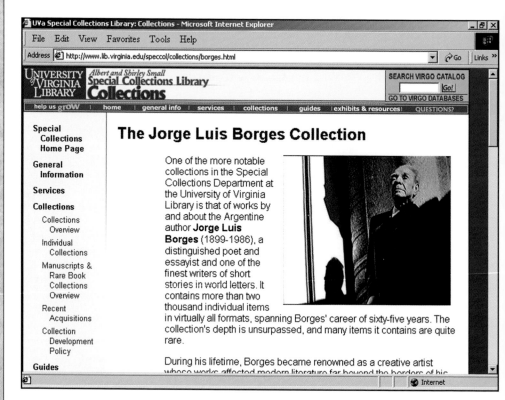

Jorge Luis Borges, recognized as one of the world's finest poets and essayists, was a native of Buenos Aires, Argentina.

Some South American artists and performers have become world famous. In the 1950s, Brazilian Carmen Miranda gained stardom with her traditional Brazilian music and dance performance. She was also known for her fancy hats adorned with tropical fruits such as pineapples and bananas. Colombian pop singer and songwriter Shakira is a current international star.

Major sports stars from South America include soccer superstar Pelé. He helped popularize the sport in North America in the 1970s. There are a growing number of South Americans playing international sports. For example, Gustavo Kuerten from Brazil is one of the world's top-ranked tennis players.

During the twentieth century, some South American writers became internationally popular. Among them were Jorge Luis Borges and Nobel prize-winning poet Gabriela Mistral from Chile. Colombian novelist Gabriel García Márquez won a Nobel Prize for literature in 1982.

In the coming years, there will likely be many more important people and celebrities in the news that were born in South America.

Chapter 2 ▶

Land and Climate

Most of South America lies between the equator and the Tropic of Capricorn, which is located 23°27′ south of the equator. This means climate conditions are mostly either tropical or subtropical. Summer temperatures average about 70°F (20°C) or higher in about three quarters of the continent. In much of this area, temperatures drop only a few degrees on average in the winter, making for very little seasonal difference. Rainfall is heavy in the low-lying tropical areas. In the south, close to the South

▲ *Workers are crossing a bridge under a waterfall in Kavac, Venezuela. The subtropical areas of South America, such as this, get plenty of rainfall.*

Pole, there is much greater variation between summer and winter temperatures. Some of the high elevations in the south have ice caps. Average annual temperatures in the southern mountains are below 50°F (10°C).[1] The giant mountain heights of the Andes in the northwest also experience colder conditions. Because much of it is south of the equator, South America has its seasons reversed from North America, Europe, and Asia.

South America's landmass is billions of years old. It was once part of a single large continent containing all the continents now in the Southern Hemisphere. Over millions of years they drifted apart. Between 15 million and 40 million years ago, South America formed its current land bridge with North America.[2]

Regions of South America

The western coast of South America consists of rugged mountains. They run from the northwest almost to the southern tip of the continent. From the northeast to the southern half of the continent, tropical forests, river valleys and plains, and coastal lowlands cover South America. The area farthest south is more diverse. It consists of mountains, wide river deltas, and fertile valleys and plateaus with moderate temperatures. Along with the seacoasts and mountain valleys of the north and central regions, the largest number of people live in the southern region of South America.

Explosive Mountains

The Andes Mountains are among the highest and most rugged in the world. A total of forty-nine mountains in South America are more than twenty thousand feet (six thousand meters) high.[3] From Chile in the South to

▲ *The Cotopaxi Volcano in Ecuador is active. Eruptions from Cotopaxi have caused mudslides that have damaged surrounding areas.*

Colombia in the North, the Andes are a major feature of South America's landscape. The Andes are also the most volcanically active mountains in the world. Major eruptions include the Cotopaxi Volcano in Ecuador in 1877 and the Villarrica Volcano in Chile in 1963. Both caused major mudslides and other damage. These volcanoes are continually active.

▶ The Tropics

The great majority of South America's land is warm and moist, typical of tropical climates. In addition to the Amazon area, lowlands near or below sea level are found in the Paraná and Uruguay River valleys in southern Brazil, Argentina, Uruguay, and Paraguay. The northeast coast of Brazil and the northern coasts of Guyana, Suriname, and French Guiana are also tropical lowlands. The rest of Guyana, Suriname, and French Guiana, as well as Venezuela and the largest part of Brazil, are at higher elevations. These regions experience subtropical climates. That means they still have warm, moist summers, but they have more seasonal changes in temperature and rainfall. The Atacama Desert in northern Chile is a region very different from most of South America. It is one of the driest places on earth. Average rainfall is only a few inches per year, and some spots have never recorded any rain at all.

Plains, Valleys, and Coasts

The southern part of South America has some very cold spots. The pampas region in Argentina and Uruguay, and the Central Valley of Chile, have temperatures between 80° and 90°F (26.7° to 32.2°C) in the summer, but average only 40° to 50°F (4.4° to 10°C) in the winter. The Patagonia region in the southernmost part of Argentina has even colder winter conditions. Two of the Andes peaks in this region have ice caps, and glaciers flow westward from here through Chile and into the Pacific Ocean. Islands at the southern tip of the continent experience some of the stormiest weather anywhere in the world. Temperatures average less than 50°F (10°C) in summer and are usually around freezing in winter. In the harshest regions, yearly rain and snow is about two hundred inches (five hundred centimeters).[4]

Along the west coast of South America, the mountains are very high, steep, and close to the ocean, where temperatures are usually warm. Elevations and temperatures vary dramatically within very short distances. "In an environment like the Andes . . . there may be three or four types of climate within a horizontal distance of only about 25 miles (40 kilometers)."[5]

Chapter 3 ▶

Plant and Animal Life

People often think of exotic tropical plants and animals when they think of South America. Indeed, the rain forests of the Amazon and other tropical areas in South America contain the greatest variety of plant and animal life on the planet. Yet there are plants and animals in South America that are very different from those found in the tropics. The other regions of South America also contain a fascinating assortment of plants and animals.

▲ The anaconda is a dangerous snake that is found in South America. Some anaconda can grow to be the same weight as adult humans or even larger.

▷ Tropical Life

South America's dense rain forests sometimes contain hundreds of tons of living plants per acre.[1] Nut, rubber, and palm trees are the most common types of trees. While they reach high into the air, a huge variety of herb plants grows closer to the ground.

Edentates are a unique kind of animal that originated in South America. Armadillos, sloths, and anteaters are all edentates. They reside mostly in the rain forest. One large kind of anteater lives mostly on open plains. One common feature that edentates have is that they are all toothless or have incomplete sets of teeth. The word edentate means "toothless."

South America is sometimes called the "bird continent." This is because nearly three thousand different species of birds are found there.[2] The tropical forest regions are especially rich in bird life. Toucans and parrots are among the many colorful species. Snake species include the boa constrictor and anaconda, whose body length and weight sometimes exceed that of many humans. Many smaller water and land snakes also flourish in the tropical forest. Vine snakes are able to blend in with the leafy vine plants that grow in the rain forest. A caecilian is a burrowing amphibian that is also unique to this kind of tropical climate.

The freshwaters of rain forest regions contain some fearsome creatures. The piranha is a carnivorous fish that lurks at the bottom of rivers and lakes and stalks prey among a wide variety of animals. Catfish in the Amazon and Orinoco rivers can grow as large as 40 pounds (18 kilograms) and sometimes attack humans. Piracucú are fish related to salmon and trout that are popular for

eating. In fact, their popularity is so great that this fish has vanished entirely from some areas.

South Americans have responded to worldwide efforts to preserve their rain forests. In 1989, the leaders of seven nations with Amazonian territory met in Brazil to discuss protecting rain forests. Afterward, Brazil's president said that the worldwide attention the issue had received had "helped to create a consciousness on the need to preserve nature."[3]

▷ The Mountains

Plant life in much of the Andes is sparse. Forests that once grew in these mountains have largely been cut down. The most common tree in the central and southern Andes is now the eucalyptus, which was brought over from Australia in the late nineteenth century. Eucalyptus is used in remedies for coughs, colds, sore throats, and to treat some infections. A very notable plant of the high Andes is the Puya raimondii. This plant is a relative of the pineapple plant. Flowers that spike from the stem of the puya can exceed thirty feet (9.1 meters) in height.

The most unique animals found in the Andes are those belonging to the Camelidae, or camel, family. Llamas originated in this area. Like donkeys, they are used by native peoples and settlers to travel through rugged mountain passages. Llamas are also used for their fur and meat. They have been exported throughout the world mostly for their soft, rich wool. Other smaller animals related to llamas that dwell in the Andes are the alpaca, guanaco, and vicuña. Vicuñas have been sought after for their fur since the Inca days. Their wool was considered so precious that in the early twentieth century, hunting almost wiped out vicuñas. Protection measures have helped vicuñas to again reproduce in large numbers.

⚠ *Llamas are still used by people living in the mountains to haul goods over dangerous mountain passes. These llamas are passing through Arequipa, Peru.*

Other animals are common in the Andes. One kind of bear lives in the Andes. Called the spectacled bear, it gets its name from its appearance of having glasses around its eyes. Big cats also live in this region, with the jaguar being the largest. Among the birds that dwell in the Andes are Andean condors. These birds are vultures (relatives of eagles and falcons) that live in rocky cliffs. They eat dead animals. Small rodents such as guinea pigs that live in the Andes provide a large portion of the condor's diet.

▷ The Galápagos

The Galápagos Islands were formed by volcanic activity off the west coast of South America. A part of the nation of Ecuador, these islands contain some of the most unique and intriguing wildlife on earth, especially giant reptiles.

The islands are named after native tortoises that weigh as much as 500 pounds (227 kilograms). Galápagos is the Spanish word for "the turtles." Iguanas on these islands are also huge, growing several feet long. Finches, a type of bird, have a heavy presence on these islands. These birds' habits vary greatly from island to island, with each finch very specifically adapted to the habitat on its particular island. Most finches eat small insects as the main part of their diet. However, on the islands with the most plant life, the finches live on seeds. One kind of finch drinks the blood of smaller land birds.

For many of the plant-eating animals on the Galápagos, the opuntia cactus plays a major role in life support. It provides fruit, nectar, and seeds for the reptiles and birds of the islands. Many kinds of sunflower plants, ranging from trees

▲ This giant dome-shaped tortoise is just one of the many interesting creatures that can be found on the Galápagos Islands.

over 40 feet (12 meters) tall to shrubs that grow only a few feet tall, have developed in the Galápagos.

Southern Region

Much of Chile and Argentina have climates and ecosystems very different from the tropical climates farther north. In the Central Valley and pampas regions, the climate is very similar to North America. Much of the forest has been cut down, but new trees have been planted. Pines and eucalyptus are most common. A tall tree called the alerce is also native to this area. The alerce can reach from 130 feet to 240 feet (40 meters to 73 meters), and some live for thousands of years. A tree called quebracho is unique to the Chaco region of northern Argentina and Paraguay. Its wood is so hard it is sometimes called the ax-breaker tree. Like many other trees in South America, this species has been heavily cut and is now rare.

Plant and animal life in southern South America is notably different from those species found in the warmer, tropical regions. A large bird called a rhea, a relative of the ostrich, lives in the central areas of Chile and Argentina. The mountain monkey, a marsupial, lives in the mountains near the southern Pacific coast. Marsupials carry their young in a pouch, just like Australian kangaroos. In southernmost South America, the climate is cold enough that only plants like moss and lichens that grow on rocks can flourish. Polar animals such as seals and penguins inhabit the rocky shorelines and islands in Patagonia and the island of Tierra del Fuego.

People and Culture

The traditions and customs of different racial and ethnic groups have blended to produce a rich culture that is distinctively South American.

▶ Europeans and American Indians Meet

The Inca had adapted many traits and skills of American Indian civilizations in South America that had preceded them. Brilliantly crafting gold into sculpture and jewelry was a specialty of the Chimú, fine pottery making a trait of the Moche, and fancy stonecutting and crafting had been a great skill of the Chavin. All these civilizations had been located in the area that the Inca would come to control.

In the east, there was not a single dominant American Indian civilization when the Portuguese first arrived. The forest-dwelling Tupi were the largest tribe. Both the Spanish and Portuguese tried to enslave American Indians to work in mines, on farms, or in the forests gathering lumber. The natives resisted forced labor, so the new settlers resorted instead to bringing African slaves to South America. Hence three distinct racial groups were brought together in large numbers in South America: Europeans, Africans, and American Indians.

▶ Cultural Blending

In South America, people from these three different races married each other. In many South American countries, there were soon large numbers of mestizos; people of

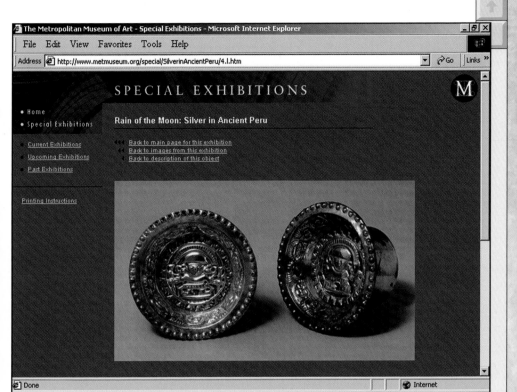

▲ *Important individuals in Andean cultures wore ear ornaments beginning in the first millennium B.C. at the earliest. Shown here are ornaments made by the Chimú of northern Peru.*

mixed European and American Indian heritage. There were also many mulattoes; people of mixed European-African descent.

This racial and cultural blending has had an enormous influence on the cultures, societies, and world image of South America. Spanish settlers built new towns and cities using European styles and techniques. Yet, the American Indian buildings and structures were so well crafted that they could not easily be destroyed. Many of today's South American towns and cities include features from both cultures.

In their weavings, sculptures, and pottery, the American Indians had often used vivid and colorful images found in nature. The mixing of European and American Indian peoples kept these artistic traditions alive in South America.

Christianity came to be the dominant religion in South America, but ancient American Indian practices did not entirely disappear. An Incan festival known as Inti Raymi (festival of the sun) continues to be celebrated every year by thousands of people in the Andean nations. People wear traditional American Indian dress and pray facing the sun. Blending of religious practices also occurred in Brazil, where African religions have coexisted and combined with Christianity. A religion called Umbanda is based upon belief in African gods and goddesses. This religion has millions of followers in Brazil.

Music is perhaps the best example of cultural blending in Brazil. Samba originated in the early nineteenth century in northeast Brazil. Along with other forms of music that developed in Brazil, it combined influences from the greatly varying cultures that came together in South America. The liner notes of the *National*

Throughout the centuries, there has been much mixing of the races in South America as natives, Europeans, and Africans came together. Shown here is a dark-skinned Brazilian woman celebrating Carnival.

Geographic Music Series claim that "Brazil's European, African, and native Indian roots are incorporated into the sounds of *samba, choro, bossa nova, forró,*—music that tells the story of this land and its people."[1]

Cultural Diversion of the South

In the southern nations of Argentina and Uruguay, the people and culture are more European. This is also true in parts of southern Brazil and Chile. More recent immigrants helped shape these places, and not all of them were Spanish or Portuguese. Large numbers of people have come from Italy, Switzerland, France, Germany, Eastern Europe, and Asia. For the most part, slaves were not imported into Argentina, Chile, or Uruguay, so these places do not have large African populations.

Many people who have come from other continents to live in South America have maintained the lifestyles of their homelands. In the Brazilian state of Santa Catarina, many German people settled and built German-style towns and businesses. A similar German culture developed in the southern Chilean city of Valdivia. A large Japanese population has settled in Brazil's São Paulo, where the Liberdade area includes hundreds of Japanese shops and restaurants. Buenos Aires and other large Argentine cities have so many people of Italian descent that the everyday language of the residents has come to be a combination of Italian and Spanish.

The Guianas

In northeastern South America lie the nations of Guyana and Suriname and an overseas department of France called French Guiana. Together they are known as the Guianas. They were all fought over by the Dutch, English, Spanish,

◁ *South American people are known for their brightly-colored traditional clothing. These people are from La Paz, Bolivia.*

and French during their early history. Guyana eventually came under British control while the Dutch held Suriname. These two countries did not gain independence until the middle of the twentieth century. They were both mostly made up of plantations. European owners brought in large numbers of African slaves and later servants from Asia to work the plantations. Asians are now a major force in Guyanese politics. Many African slaves in Suriname escaped from their plantations and formed colonies in the dense jungle. Along with American Indians in Suriname, many of these Africans, called bushland people, continue to live independently in remote areas. They rely mostly on hunting, fishing, and nomadic agriculture for survival.

France also brought in slaves from Africa and workers from Asia to French Guiana. Yet the greatest number of people in this territory are of French heritage. There has not been the kind of racial and cultural blending in the Guianas that has occurred in most of South America. The official languages are English in Guyana, Dutch in Suriname, and French in French Guiana.

Economy

South America has been known for a great variety of products and resources. Minerals, crops, lumber, meat, and fish are some of the most important aspects of South America's economy. Throughout its history, South America has had a big gap between its richest and poorest citizens. The products and industries that South America has depended on have greatly contributed to this inequality.

▷ Mines, Forests, and the First Farms

The first Spanish settlers in western South America set their sights on mining precious metals in the mountains,

▲ This is an image of land that has been used for cast-iron mining in Brazil. Mining is still an important part of the overall South American economy.

especially gold and silver. Portuguese explorers and settlers craved the Brazil wood trees in Brazil. These were used to craft great artworks and make red dye that was treasured by nobles in Europe. Precious metals were later discovered in the western mountains of Brazil. The high value of these South American resources led to severe exploitation of both the land and the native peoples in the area. Soon large plantations that raised crops such as sugar cane appeared.

The labor required to grow large sugar crops led to large-scale importation of African slaves to South America. Brazil was an especially big importer of African slaves. About 4 million slaves are estimated to have been brought into Brazil between the sixteenth and nineteenth centuries.[1]

The wealth created by these plantations went mostly to their European owners. Slavery was outlawed in all South American nations during the nineteenth century, but illegal slavery continued in some places. Foreigners could still be brought in as workers in debt to their bosses. Many workers were kept in poverty working as sharecroppers. This meant that they depended upon the crops they grew and a share of the money brought in from those crops for their survival. It was in this way that coffee bean production later became a huge part of South America's economy.

Another product that led to abuse of land and native peoples was rubber produced from rubber trees in the Amazon River region. Tribes living in the rain forest had their lives disrupted by the destruction of their environment. Rubber harvesting paid them very low wages while rubber company owners, most of whom were foreign, earned huge profits. Rubber became a major export from rain forest areas during the early 1900s. However, when Asian nations also began producing rubber in the 1920s, South America's rubber industry collapsed.

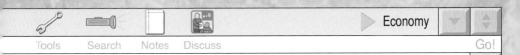

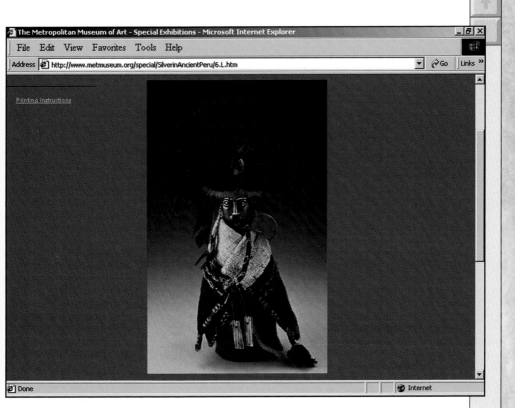

The Metropolitan Museum of Art - Special Exhibitions - Microsoft Internet Explorer

File   Edit   View   Favorites   Tools   Help

Address http://www.metmuseum.org/special/SilverinAncientPeru/6.L.htm   Go   Links

Printing Instructions

Done   Internet

△ *This figurine, a gift to the Inca mountain gods, was buried in Chile alongside a nine-year-old boy. The body of the figure is made of silver and is dressed in female garb except for its feather headdress. Silver has been a precious metal to South Americans for hundreds of years.*

The mining of gold, silver, and diamonds also declined greatly in South America when these materials were depleted. However, mining has remained a major industry. Tin, copper, and iron ore are still important exports for many South American countries.

▷ Diverse Agriculture and Manufacturing

As farming became more widespread in South America, the more temperate, flat, and open regions became major food producers. The pampas region in Argentina and Uruguay

became a major cattle-breeding area. Argentina is now one of the major producers of beef for worldwide consumption. The Central Valley of Chile and the north-central regions of Argentina both produce a wide variety of grains, vegetables, and fruits. These range from corn, wheat, and potatoes to plums, nectarines, and grapes for making fine wines. Tropical fruits such as bananas, mangoes, and papayas are widely grown in South America. Fruits and vegetables grown on the continent are shipped throughout the world. Fish and seafood are also major exports of some countries. Cacao plants, used to produce chocolate, are commonly grown in the northern mountain regions.

Another product that was distinctive to this area at one time was guano, or solid bird waste droppings. Massive amounts of this substance would pile up in areas where large flocks of birds gathered. Shipping of guano to Europe for fertilizer was an especially big part of the economies of Peru and Bolivia in the nineteenth century.

Manufacturing became a major part of South America's economy during the twentieth century. Processed food products, cement, and medical drugs are among South America's major manufactured products. Argentina, Brazil, and Venezuela have large car-manufacturing industries. Oil, natural gas, and coal, all energy resources, have emerged in the twentieth century as important aspects of South America's economy. Venezuela is a leading oil producer. It was the single biggest oil-exporting nation in the world from 1929 until 1970.[2]

▶ Welcoming the World

Tourism is one way in which many South American nations are improving their economies. Ancient native ruins and early Spanish colonial buildings attract a lot of

▲ *The ruins of Machu Picchu are one of the most popular tourist destinations in Peru. Tourism is helping South American nations improve their economies.*

tourists. Many people are also interested in seeing the natural beauty of the tropical rain forests and the Andes Mountains. Ecuador's Galápagos Islands draw visitors to see their rare and unusual creatures. This interest in the natural beauty of South America's unique environments also helps to promote environmental preservation.

The Patagonia Mountains in the south are increasingly popular for skiing and other winter sports. Festivals such as Carnival attract millions of people from around the world to Rio de Janeiro and other Brazilian cities. Buenos Aires in Argentina is also world famous for its lively nightlife. Many people visit that city every year for its restaurants, theaters, and music and dance clubs.

Exploration and History

The first people journeyed to South America about twelve thousand years ago. Like early inhabitants of North America, it is believed most came over a land bridge from Asia during the Ice Age. There is evidence that the inhabitants on Easter Island off the coast of Chile first came in boats from islands in the South Pacific. These people hunted, gathered wild

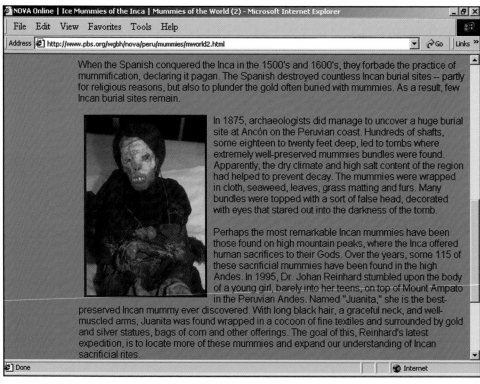

NOVA Online | Ice Mummies of the Inca | Mummies of the World (2) - Microsoft Internet Explorer

File   Edit   View   Favorites   Tools   Help

Address http://www.pbs.org/wgbh/nova/peru/mummies/mworld2.html

When the Spanish conquered the Inca in the 1500's and 1600's, they forbade the practice of mummification, declaring it pagan. The Spanish destroyed countless Incan burial sites -- partly for religious reasons, but also to plunder the gold often buried with mummies. As a result, few Incan burial sites remain.

In 1875, archaeologists did manage to uncover a huge burial site at Ancón on the Peruvian coast. Hundreds of shafts, some eighteen to twenty feet deep, led to tombs where extremely well-preserved mummies bundles were found. Apparently, the dry climate and high salt content of the region had helped to prevent decay. The mummies were wrapped in cloth, seaweed, leaves, grass matting and furs. Many bundles were topped with a sort of false head, decorated with eyes that stared out into the darkness of the tomb.

Perhaps the most remarkable Incan mummies have been those found on high mountain peaks, where the Inca offered human sacrifices to their Gods. Over the years, some 115 of these sacrificial mummies have been found in the high Andes. In 1995, Dr. Johan Reinhard stumbled upon the body of a young girl, barely into her teens, on top of Mount Ampato in the Peruvian Andes. Named "Juanita," she is the best-preserved Incan mummy ever discovered. With long black hair, a graceful neck, and well-muscled arms, Juanita was found wrapped in a cocoon of fine textiles and surrounded by gold and silver statues, bags of corn and other offerings. The goal of this, Reinhard's latest expedition, is to locate more of these mummies and expand our understanding of Incan sacrificial rites.

Done   Internet

▲ *The Chinchorro lived along the northern coast of what is now Chile. They are thought to be the first people to embalm their dead. Mummies of this tribe date back to 5000 B.C. Shown here is Juanita, an embalmed Inca girl in her early teens who was sacrificed to the gods.*

food, and wandered until around 5000 B.C., when the first villages and farming settlements appeared. A succession of civilized peoples, centered in the northwest Andes, followed. The Chavin people first appeared around 1000 B.C. They shared many characteristics with the Nazca, Moche, Tiahuanaca, and Chimú civilizations that followed them. The Chimú were the ruling tribal group in much of South America in the fifteenth century before being conquered by the Inca in 1476.

The Inca conquered many other rivals, though not all of them. Dense tropical forests protected some tribes from the large Incan armies. The Araucanian people in southern Chile defeated the Inca in battle to defend their territory. However, the Inca became the most dominant precolonial people of South America. They reached their height under the successive leadership of Pachacuti and his descendants, Topa Inca and Huayna Capac, between 1438 and 1525. These rulers claimed to be descended from ancient gods and were revered by the Inca people.

▶ Spanish and Portuguese Colonies

Spanish explorers had traveled south from the Caribbean, Mexico, and Central America. The first Spanish expedition into South America was led by Pascual de Andagoya in 1522. This was followed by an expedition by Francisco Pizarro in 1527. In 1532, Pizarro returned to South America to conquer the mighty Inca Empire. He succeeded in doing this in spite of being overwhelmingly outnumbered. With only 168 men, Pizarro conquered an Incan army of tens of thousands. He did this by luring the Inca leader Atahualpa into an ambush. Pizarro took Atahualpa hostage and killed thousands of Incan troops in a surprise attack. So stunning was Pizarro's victory that it has been described as "the most

peru, 9 - Microsoft Internet Explorer

File　Edit　View　Favorites　Tools　Help

Address http://www.tribalarts.com/feature/peru/peru09.html

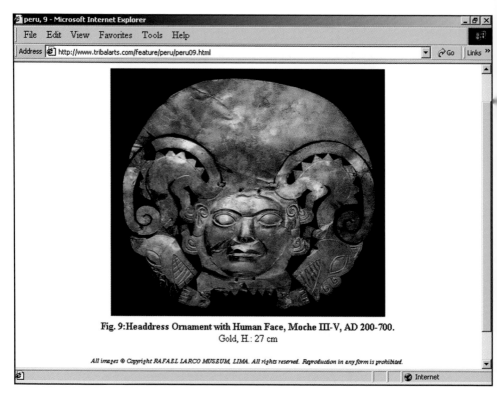

Fig. 9:Headdress Ornament with Human Face, Moche III-V, AD 200-700.
Gold, H.: 27 cm

▲ *The Moche tribe used art to show man's relationship with nature by incorporating both human and animal aspects.*

astonishing military feat in history."[1] The Inca tried to pay for their leader's freedom, but Pizarro had Atahualpa killed.

Pizarro and the Spaniards claimed control over the Inca Empire. Spanish America was divided into regions called viceroyalties. These territories developed into what are now the nine nations of Spanish South America.

Portuguese explorers looking for routes to Asia were the first to visit Brazil. Vasco da Gama sailed around the southern tip of South America, called Cape Horn, during a trip to India in 1498. Another Portuguese explorer, Pedro Alvares Cabral, set foot upon Brazil and passed word back to the Portuguese kingdom about the land he had found. Many more Portuguese came to explore Brazil and build settlements. They sought to keep strong trade routes to Asia and make use of the natural resources of the newly discovered land.

The Portuguese government began a system of local governments called captaincies in 1534. There were twelve captaincies established at that time. Eventually, Brazil would grow into a nation with twenty-six separate states.

Other Colonies and Settlements

While colonies were firmly established under Spanish and Portuguese control in the sixteenth century, control over the Guianas was not settled until the nineteenth century. The British gained control of Guyana in 1814. Suriname was ceded to the Dutch by the British in 1667 in exchange for the North American colony of New York, but the British retook control of Suriname for twenty years in the eighteenth and nineteenth centuries. Suriname came under Dutch control for good in 1816. French Guiana was alternately under Dutch, French, and combined British-Portuguese control until 1816. The Falkland Islands, off the Atlantic coast of Argentina, were fought over by Spain, France, England, and later the new South American nation of Argentina. These islands have remained under British control since 1834, but their ownership is still disputed by Argentina.

South American Independence

Independence for Spanish America came largely from growing unhappiness among those living in the American colonies under Spanish rule. In the eighteenth century, Spaniards who had been born in America (called Creoles) came to resent European-born Spaniards (called Peninsulars).

Peninsulars enjoyed power and privileges in Spanish America that the Creoles did not. Many people born in the colonies were educated in Europe in the eighteenth century. At that time, well-known writers and philosophers were putting forth ideas about freedom and representative government. Educated Spanish Americans also knew about the revolutions against the British in the United States and against the royal government of France. A growing number of Creoles and other people of various racial backgrounds in Spanish America became interested in gaining independence from Spain and governing themselves.

Two people who supported independence for Spanish South America were José de San Martín and Simón Bolívar. These men led armies fighting for independence

▲ Simón Bolívar was a key figure in helping the people of South America gain independence from their colonial rulers. This man is passing by a mural of Bolívar on a street in Caracas, Venezuela.

against Spanish forces. The first revolutionary groups formed in Venezuela, Colombia, Chile, and Argentina. San Martín led revolutionary forces from Argentina while Bolívar fought for independence in the northern countries. The fighting between Spanish and South American forces lasted almost fifteen years. Bolívar led the American forces to victory in 1824, gaining legendary status as the founder of South American independence from Spain.

In Brazil, opposition to Portuguese rule in the early nineteenth century was not as intense. A good part of the reason was that the Portuguese ruler and many Portuguese nobles moved to the Brazilian city of Rio de Janeiro in 1807. This occurred after Portugal was invaded and conquered by French armies led by Napoléon. Crown Prince Dom João kept the Portuguese government in exile in Rio de Janeiro. He became king of both Portugal and Brazil in 1816 and remained in Brazil even after Napoleon's forces had been driven out of Portugal. João came to have a fondness for the people of Brazil. He also showed he had more understanding of South American's desire for independence than the rulers of Spain. When João finally returned to Portugal in 1821, he left his son Dom Pedro as ruler of Brazil. João told Pedro that, if Brazil were to demand independence, "proclaim it yourself and put the crown on your own head."[2]

Pedro did that just one year later, and Portugal did not try to prevent national independence in South America as Spain had done. Unlike the countries that emerged in Spanish South America, Brazil kept a monarchy for a government. Pedro ruled as king until 1831, when his son took over. Pedro II was finally removed from power in 1889, when Brazil became a republic.

▶ International Wars

There have been several wars between nations of South America. Argentina and Brazil went to war in the 1820s over a disputed territory, the Banda Oriental. Inhabitants of this area were Spanish speaking, but Brazil occupied the area in 1817. Britain, which had a strong trading interest with both nations, arranged an agreement that led to the creation of the nation of Uruguay out of the territory. Chile has gone to war twice with Peru and Bolivia, in the 1830s and again in the 1880s. Competition over territory along the Pacific coast drove those wars. Chile was victorious in both wars. In the second of those wars, called the War of the Pacific, Bolivia lost its only coastal territory, the Atacama Desert, to Chile.

The two most violent wars in South American history have both involved Paraguay. The War of the Triple Alliance started in 1864 between Paraguay and the allied nations of Brazil, Argentina, and Uruguay. Overall, the combined forces of those three countries were vastly superior to those of Paraguay. Paraguay, though, was led by a great military and inspirational ruler, Francisco Solano López. He and his troops invaded parts of Argentina and Brazil to start the war. They later successfully defended themselves from armies that moved against them and into Paraguay. The war lasted for six years, killing hundreds of thousands, including about 90 percent of Paraguay's male population.[3] Another war was fought in the 1930s, this one between Paraguay and Bolivia, over territory in the fertile Chaco area. Between the two nations, close to a hundred thousand people died in this war.

In 1982, Argentina, under the leadership of a military government, attacked the Falkland Islands, a British colony. Argentina claimed rights to the islands, which they called the Malvinas. This was based on Spanish claims to the islands dating back to the mid-eighteenth century. Argentina invaded and occupied West Falkland Island but was driven out by British forces within a few weeks.

Internal Conflicts

More central to South American history than wars between countries has been conflict within countries, including civil wars and uprisings. These have often resulted from struggle and conflict between people of different economic classes.

Argentina faced almost forty years of civil conflict after declaring its independence. Some people wanted to keep local governments separate from the national government based in Buenos Aires. These people fought against the

▲ This image shows the Villarrica Volcano, located in Pucon, Chile, and the valley below. As South American countries continue developing their abundant natural resources, the result will be a better life for the people who live there.

new national government. Many wealthy landowners thought they would make more money under smaller local governments instead of a single national government. Colombia has been plagued with civil conflict during much of its history. The War of a Thousand Days was a civil war fought between conservative and liberal factions within Colombia. The conflict was fought between 1899 and 1901. Tens of thousands died in that war and there was massive destruction to the country. Another civil conflict of the twentieth century known as La Violencia caused massive loss of life and devastation in Colombia.

Other countries in South America were more stable early in their histories. Among these were Brazil, Peru, and Chile. Each of these established democratic governments soon after independence. However, even in democratic South American countries the wealthy had great advantages. Voting rights were usually granted only to those who could read and write and who owned land. As more people moved into the middle class and industrial laborers joined forces in union and political activity, civil conflicts between rich and poor increased.

Class conflicts in South America took on international interest during the Cold War between the Western powers and communist countries in the twentieth century. Communist countries provided support to rebel movements and guerrilla armies in many countries, including Brazil, Argentina, Peru, and Colombia. The United States supported military overthrows of communist leaders. Sometimes this policy did not work out well for the South American people. One such incident was a leader named General Augusto Pinochet Ugarte, whom the United States helped to overthrow the government of Chile. Pinochet proved to be a ruthless and brutal leader.

People celebrating Carnival in Recife, Brazil.

Signs for the Future

By the beginning of the twenty-first century, elected leaders headed all South American nations. There were many efforts to improve economic conditions and preserve the continent's vast natural treasures. However, there were also signs that the problems that had long afflicted South America had not totally disappeared. In 2002, Venezuelan President Hugo Chávez was removed in a military coup. Chávez enacted sweeping economic reforms that were very unpopular with the upper and middle classes. Following Chávez's removal, his supporters took to the streets and forced the new leader to resign. Low-level members of the military returned Chávez to power just two days after his removal. This conflict continued to plague Venezuela at the start of 2004.

Progress is being made in most places in South America. Natural resources throughout the continent are plentiful, and South American countries are learning to develop them. The standard of living in most places is improving, and there are growing numbers of middle-class professionals and skilled workers. These things have provided South Americans with hope for a bright future.

Chapter 1. A Colorful Place

1. Rex A. Hudson, ed., *Peru: A Country Study,* Library of Congress Country Studies, 1992, <http://lcweb2.loc.gov/cgi-bin/query/r?frd/cstdy: @field(DOCID+pe0014)> (March 1, 2004).

2. John Charles Chasteen, *Born in Blood and Fire: A Concise History of Latin America* (New York: W.W. Norton & Company, 2001), p. 318.

Chapter 2. Land and Climate

1. Simon Collier, Harold Blakemore, and Thomas E. Skidmore, eds., *The Cambridge Encyclopedia of Latin America and the Caribbean* (Cambridge, UK: Cambridge University Press, 1985), p. 19.

2. Ibid., p. 16.

3. Staff, *World Almanac and Book of Facts 2002* (New York: World Almanac Books, 2002), p. 453.

4. Collier et al., eds., pp. 21–23.

5. Ibid., p. 21.

Chapter 3. Plant and Animal Life

1. Simon Collier, Harold Blakemore, and Thomas E. Skidmore, eds., *The Cambridge Encyclopedia of Latin America and the Caribbean* (Cambridge, UK: Cambridge University Press, 1985), p. 30.

2. Ibid., p. 29.

3. James Barnham, "South America Summit Agrees To Save Rain Forest," *Financial Times,* May 8, 1989, p. 4.

Chapter 4. People and Culture

1. Josh Yafa, Liner notes to "Destination Brazil," compact disc, *National Geographic,* 2001.

Chapter 5. Economy

1. Boris Fausto, *A Concise History of Brazil* (Cambridge, UK: Cambridge University Press, 1999), p. 18.

2. Richard A. Haggerty, ed., "Venezuela: A Country Study," *Library of Congress Country Studies,* 1990, <http://lcweb2.loc.gov/cgi-bin/query/r?frd/ cstdy:@field(DOCID+ve0051)> (March 1, 2004).

Chapter 6. Exploration and History

1. Michael Hart, *The 100: A Ranking of the Most Influential Persons in History* (New York: Galahad Books, 1982), p. 347.

2. John A. Crow, *The Epic of Latin America,* 4th ed. (Berkeley: University of California Press, 1992), p. 526.

3. Simon Collier, Harold Blakemore, and Thomas E. Skidmore, eds., *The Cambridge Encyclopedia of Latin America and the Caribbean* (Cambridge, UK: Cambridge University Press, 1985), pp. 288–290.

Further Reading

Bramwell, Martyn. *Central and South America.* Minneapolis, Minn.: Lerner Publications, 2000.

Corona, Laurel. *Brazil.* San Diego, Calif.: Lucent Books, 2000.

De Varona, Frank. *Simón Bolívar: Latin American Liberator.* Brookfield, Conn.: Millbrook Press, 1993.

Dwyer, Christopher. *Chile.* New York: Chelsea House, 1990.

Hintz, Martin. *Argentina.* New York: Children's Press, 1998.

Martell, Hazel Mary. *Civilizations of Peru Before 1535.* Austin, Tex.: Raintree Steck-Vaughn, 1999.

McLeish, Ewan. *South America.* Austin, Tex.: Raintree Steck-Vaughn, 1997.

Morrison, Marion. *Peru.* New York: Children's Press, 2000.

Myers, Lynn Born and Christopher A. *Galápagos: Islands of Change.* New York: Hyperion Books, 1995.

Pollard, Michael. *The Amazon.* Tarrytown, N.Y.: Marshall Cavendish Corporation, 1998.

Selba, Anna. *Argentina, Chile, Paraguay, Uruguay.* Austin, Tex.: Raintree Steck-Vaughn, 1999.

Wardrope, William. *Venezuela.* Milwaukee, Wis.: Gareth Stevens, 2003.

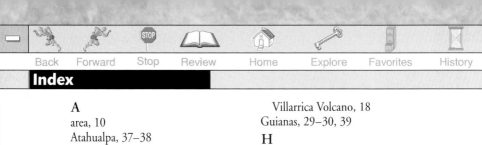